MW00931900

Lands of Grass

By Allan Fowler

Consultants
Linda Cornwell, Coordinator of School Quality
and Professional Improvement
Indiana State Teachers Association

Janann V. Jenner, Ph.D.

Children's Press®
A Division of Grolier Publishing
New York   London   Hong Kong   Sydney
Danbury, Connecticut

Visit Children's Press® on the Internet at:
http://publishing.grolier.com

Designer: Herman Adler Design Group
Photo Researcher: Caroline Anderson

The photo on the cover of this book shows a grassland east of the
Rocky Mountains in the United States.

Library of Congress Cataloging-in-Publication Data

Fowler, Allan.
    Lands of grass / by Allan Fowler.
       p. cm. — (Rookie read-about science)
    Includes index.
    Summary: Describes grassland ecosystems and the animals found there,
including prairies, steppes, and savannas.
    ISBN 0-516-21213-3 (lib. bdg.)   0-516-27089-3 (pbk.)
    1. Grassland ecology Juvenile literature. [1. Grasslands. 2. Grassland
ecology. 3. Ecology.] I. Title. II. Series.
QH541.5.P7F68   2000   99-32313
577.4—dc21   CIP
                                                                     AC

Badlands National Park, South Dakota

In some parts of the world, grass covers large areas of land.

Grande Serto Veredas National Park in Brazil, a country in South America

Shrubs and flowers may grow in these grasslands, but there are few trees.

There are many different
kinds of grasslands.

Prairies have tall grass,
wildflowers, and a few
scattered trees.

Purple cornflowers growing on a prairie.

A prairie in winter

Prairies have hot summers and cold, snowy winters.

In spring and fall, prairies get a lot of rain.

Steppes (STEPS) have short grass. The grass is not as thick as grass on prairies. This is because steppes get less rain.

A steppe in Arizona

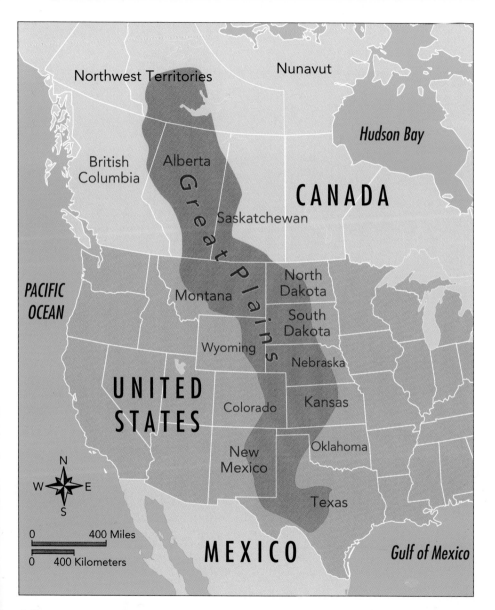

Northwest Territories

Nunavut

Hudson Bay

British Columbia

Alberta

Great Plains

CANADA

Saskatchewan

PACIFIC OCEAN

Montana

North Dakota

South Dakota

Wyoming

Nebraska

UNITED STATES

Colorado

Kansas

New Mexico

Oklahoma

Texas

N
W   E
S

0   400 Miles

0   400 Kilometers

MEXICO

Gulf of Mexico

One very large steppe is called the Great Plains.

It stretches from the Northwest Territories of Canada to Texas.

Many kinds of animals live
on prairies and steppes.
There are bison or buffalo,
deer, foxes, prairie dogs,
mice, and all sorts of birds
and insects.

Bison

Red fox

A savannah in South America

16

Savannahs are large, flat grasslands with clumps of trees and shrubs.

They are found in parts of Africa, Australia, India, and South America.

A savannah in Kenya, a country in Africa

Herds of zebras, gazelles, giraffes, elephants, and other grass-eaters live on the savannahs of Africa.

African elephants

A savannah in Botswana, a country in Africa

Savannahs are hot all year long. They have one rainy season and one dry season.

Some areas that were once covered with grasslands are now used for farming.

A cornfield in Nebraska

A wheat field in Alberta, Canada

The great wheat fields and cornfields of the North American Midwest used to be natural grasslands.

In a way, they still are grasslands. Wheat and corn are kinds of grass.

Other grasslands are
perfect for grazing
cattle and sheep.

Shepherds wander
the steppes of Asia
with their flocks.

Cattle grazing on a grassland

Most of the grasslands that once grew on Earth are gone. Towns and cities have been built on them.

Juniata, Nebraska

A grassland in Nebraska

We must protect the
grasslands that are left.

Words You Know

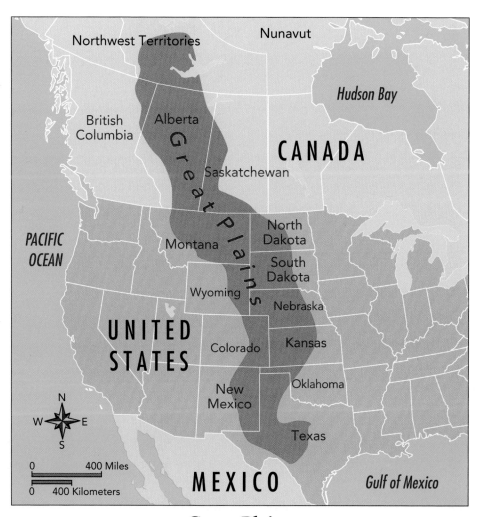

Great Plains

bison

herd

savannah

grassland

prairie

steppe

31

Index

About the Author

Allan Fowler is a freelance writer with a background in advertising. Born in New York, he now lives in Chicago and enjoys traveling.

Photo Credits

©: Photo Researchers: 14, 31 top left (Tim Davis), 4 (Fletcher & Baylis), 27 (David R. Frazier), 23 (Jeff Greenberg), 19, 31 center left (Clem Haagner), 15 (Tom & Pat Leeson), 24 (David Nunuk/SPL), 3, 8, 31 top right (Rod Planck), 7, 31 center right (Richard E. Trump); Visuals Unlimited: 11, 31 bottom right (Walt Anderson), cover (Don W. Fawcett), 16, 31 bottom left (Geoge Loun), 18 (Joe McDonald), 20 (Charles McRae), 28, 29 (William J. Weber).

Map by Joan McEvoy.